Fancywork and Fashion's

# Action Wear for Dolls

## By Joan Hinds and Jean Becker

A Book of Five Sewing Patterns
for 18" Dolls On the Go

**ISBN 0-9636287-4-7**

Copyright 1996 by Fancywork and Fashion. All rights reserved.
No portion of this book may be reproduced without
written permission of the publisher.

**Fancywork and Fashion Press**
**Duluth, Minnesota**

# FOREWORD

We're pretty nostalgic about the good old days, when we were little kids. And that's been reflected in our design work. In fact, we've wallowed in the '50s quite a bit in our previous pattern books.

But things weren't perfect then either. For instance, girls had to wear dresses to school every day. (In our climate, that was downright ridiculous!)

And gym class, well, that was a joke. We barely worked up a glow, let alone a sweat. The boys played basketball; we had sessions on good grooming. And worst of all, if we ever wanted to wear a letter jacket, we had to have a boyfriend who was an athlete.

Yes, a lot of things are better nowadays. Our daughters don't freeze their kneecaps off waiting for the bus because now they're wearing overalls and blue jeans. They're entitled to participate in the same sports as the boys, sometimes even on the same teams. And best of all, they get to earn their own letter jackets, whether for athletics, music or academics.

Girls still play with dolls, though, and the most popular kind today are 18" vinyl child dolls. And they need their own action wear! These outfits require more steps than most of our previous designs, but they're still basic sewing and our instructions are easy to follow. Dust off that sewing machine and save yourself some money by making these costumes yourself.

We'd like to acknowledge the design assistance of our friends Karen Cermak and Lauri Cushing. And thanks to all our loyal readers who share their helpful hints and funny stories about their lives with dolls.

**Joan Hinds**                                **Jean Becker**

# INTRODUCTION

These patterns are designed to fit 18" modern vinyl dolls. But we all know that height alone does not determine fit of a costume. Different brands of dolls have slightly different body types. To further compound the problem, we have found that individual dolls within a single brand vary quite a bit in the amount of stuffing used, resulting in different waist measurements.

The most common waist measurement among our cloth-bodied vinyl dolls is 11", so that is the standard used in our pattern pieces. Please measure your doll's waist before you begin sewing to make sure you do not need to make adjustments. We know people who have performed surgery on their doll rather than alter a pattern; but trust us--it's really much easier to lengthen or shorten waistbands and elastic than resort to such drastic remedies!

Secondly, please remember that **our doll costume patterns, like most on the market, use a 1/4" seam allowance**. They are included in the pattern pieces, though they are not drawn on. If you should forget and use 5/8" seam allowances, your outfits will end up too small.

Third, remember to have fun. Hobbies are supposed to relax you, not put more pressure on you. Take your time and enjoy the process as well as the result.

# English Riding Costume With Helmet

*Nearly every young girl goes through an "I love horses!" phase. Most aren't lucky enough to actually get those riding lessons, but we can dream, can't we? This outfit emulates the United States Equestrian Team's uniform at the 1996 Summer Olympics. It has a lot of pattern pieces and instructions, but is not really an advanced project. Step-by-step instructions will lead you to a very rewarding result.*

### Supplies

**Blouse and Jabot**
    1/4 yd. white broadcloth
    3 snaps

**Breeches**
    1/3 yd. white cotton/Lycra® knit
    2" Velcro® strip

**Jacket**
    1/4 yd. red wool
    Scrap of blue velveteen for collar
    Scrap of blue lining for collar
    Three 3/8" gold shank-style buttons
    3 snaps

**Helmet**
    1/4 yd. black velveteen
    1/4 yd. heavy interfacing
    16" black single-fold bias tape
    One 3/4" covered button form

### BLOUSE

1. This is a self-lined, sleeveless shell. Cut out two fronts and four backs.

2. On grain, cut a strip of broadcloth 1-1/4" X 8" for the collar.

3. Sew front to backs at shoulder seams. Repeat for lining.

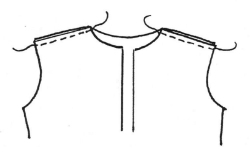

4. Right sides together, sew lining to blouse at center back seams. Likewise, stitch around the armholes. Clip curves and turn right side out.

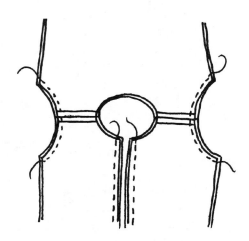

5. Press one long edge of the collar up 1/4". Pin unfolded long edge of the collar around the blouse neckline **on the wrong side**, with the short ends of the collar extending 1/4" beyond the center backs of the blouse. Stitch.

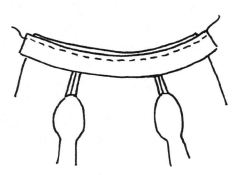

6. Fold the short ends in and fold the collar over to the outside of the garment. From the right side, stitch around the collar on the right side.

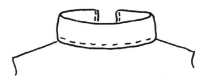

7. Right sides together, sew underarm seam. Hem lower edge of blouse by pressing it up 1/4" and stitching.

8. Lapping right over left, sew three snaps to center back of blouse.

## JABOT

1. Cut a strip of broadcloth 1-3/4" X 17". Narrow hem all edges. Tie around neck with single loop.

## BREECHES

1. Cut two along fold line. Right sides together, sew center back seam.

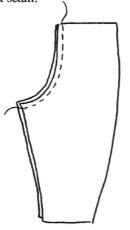

2. Sew center front seam up to dot. Serge or zig-zag seam allowances all the way to the waist.

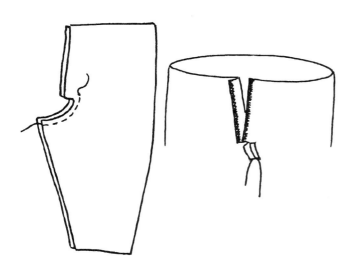

3. Press left front toward inside of garment along seam line and baste at waistline. Zig-zag or serge around waist of breeches. Press toward inside of garment 1/4" and topstitch.

4. Serge or zig-zag lower edges of pants. Turn up 1/4" and topstitch.

5. Right sides together, sew inner leg seam.

6. Cut Velcro® in half lengthwise and sew this narrow strip of it to the center fronts of the breeches, curving the stitching line so that it looks like a real fly.

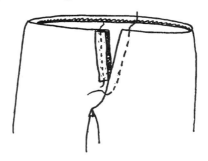

## JACKET

1. This is an unlined jacket. It has a lot of steps, but it's all basic sewing. Cut two fronts, two backs, two sleeves and two neck facings from the wool.

2. Stitch the dart in each back.

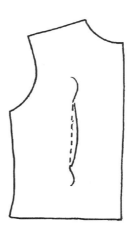

3. Right sides together, sew the center back seam from the neckline down to the dot. Carefully press the seam allowances open from the inside of the garment. Remember this is wool and needs a lower temperature on your iron. Top stitch around the back vent.

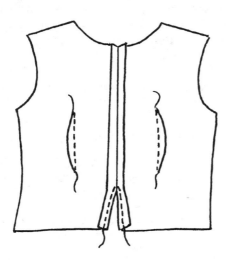

4. For pockets, cut two squares of wool 3" X 3". Fold them in half right sides together so they measure 1-1/2" X 3". Sew one short end of each pocket and turn it right side out.

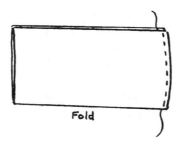

5. Place the long unfolded edge of the pocket flap along the pocket stitching line marked on the jacket front pattern piece. Stitch 1/4" from the raw edge of the pocket flap.

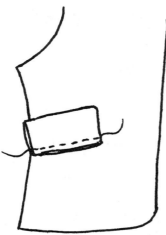

6. Fold the pocket flap down and baste the short unstitched edge along the jacket side seam line. Hand stitch the other corner of pocket flap in place on the jacket as shown.

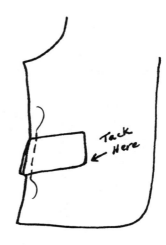

7. Zig-zag or serge the lower edges of the jacket. Do not hem yet.

8. Right sides together, sew shoulder seams.

9. Cut out collar and collar lining. Right sides together, sew collar to lining along short ends and along one long edge (not the neckline edge). Trim seams, clip curves and turn right side out. Press from wrong side.

10. Pin collar to right side of jacket, matching center of collar to center back seam of jacket. Baste in place.

11. Right sides together, sew center back seam of jacket facing. Press seam allowance open. Serge or zig-zag the long inside edge of the facing as shown.

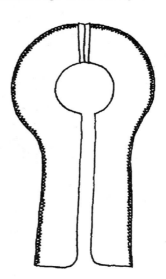

12. Right sides together, pin jacket facing to jacket, sandwiching the collar in between the jacket and the facing. Stitch across the lower end of the facing, up the center front, around the neckline, down the other center front and across the remaining short end of the facing. Clip corners and curves, trim seam allowances and turn right side out. Press gently from wrong side.

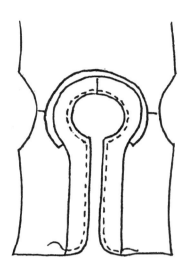

13. Understitch the facing to the jacket around the neckline to anchor the facing. This will not show when the collar is laid back down again.

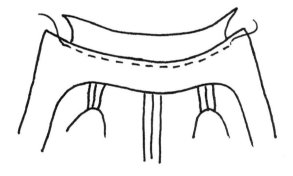

14. Zig-zag or serge the bottom edges of the sleeves. Hem by pressing under 1/4" and hand stitching.

15. Gather the sleeve cap slightly. Right sides together, pin to armhole of jacket. Stitch.

16. Right sides together and starting at wrist, sew sleeve and jacket underarm seam all at once. Clip curves. Turn right side out.

17. To hem, press the lower edges of the jacket under 1/4" and top stitch from the beginning of the jacket facings to the center back vent. To keep them in place, tack the jacket lapels to the jacket. Stitch 3 buttons to the right front as indicated on the pattern piece. Sew snaps underneath.

**HELMET**

1. This "helmet" is really more of a hat, but you wouldn't really want to deal with hard plastic, would you? Cut four crown pieces from the velveteen and four from the heavy interfacing. Cut two brims from the velveteen and one from the interfacing. Notice they have different cutting lines.

2. Baste an interfacing piece to the wrong side of each velveteen crown piece. Leave the brims alone for now.

3. Right sides together, sew the four crown seams. Press the seam allowances open.

4. Baste the interfacing brim to the wrong side of one velveteen brim only along the inner curve. Right sides together, sew the interfaced brim to the remaining brim around the **outside** curved seam. Be sure not to catch the interfacing in the seam. Clip seam allowances and turn right side out.

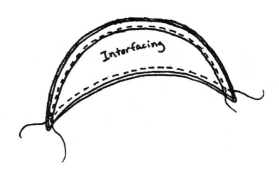

5. Right sides together, center the brim along one section of the crown and pin it in place. Stitch.

6. Right sides together and raw edges flush, pin the bias tape all around the bottom of the helmet, sandwiching the brim in between and overlapping the ends of the tape. Stitch.

7. Trim seam allowances. Fold the bias tape toward the inside of the helmet. Topstitch all around the crown just above the seam line, sewing through all layers to hold the bias tape in place.

8. Following the button form instructions, cover it with velveteen. Sew to top of helmet.

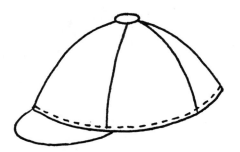

# Marching Band Uniform

**Supplies for Pants**

1/3 yd. black twill or gabardine
2/3 yd. of 3/8" grosgrain ribbon same color
    as jacket

**Supplies for Jacket**

1/3 yd. colored twill or gabardine
4 snaps or Velcro® strips

**Supplies for Overlay**

1/4 yd. white twill or gabardine
Scrap of black twill or gabardine
    for collar
Scrap of colored twill or gabardine
    for back of overlay
Scrap of colored felt for school symbol
4" of 7/8" wide black grosgrain ribbon
8" of 1" wide colored grosgrain ribbon
20" of 3/8" wide colored grosgrain ribbon
15" of 5/8" wide white grosgrain ribbon
12" of 5/8" wide red grosgrain ribbon
2/3 yd. white cording (1/4" wide)
Scrap of black felt for letters
1-1/2" tall felt iron-on letters
1" strip of Velcro®
2 pairs of half-rings (5/8" wide) for belt

**Supplies for Hat**

1 sheet (11" X 14") white posterboard
1/4 yd. white fabric-backed
    leather-look vinyl
1 square red felt
14" white soutache braid
2 (1/2") silver buttons
6" of silver chain, about 3/16" diameter
Gold foil starburst (from Christmas ornament)
    or other similar metallic-look emblem
One feather (optional)

*Okay, we admit the supplies list is rather daunting. But this really isn't very difficult sewing. It just has a lot of detail work, and that's the creative part that we all love so much. You can customize this uniform to match your local school's colors and symbols. When we refer to "colored twill" or "colored ribbon" we are talking about the main color--in our case, red. Your school will be different. The uniform shown is a duplicate of the one worn by Joan's son Kevin, at Duluth Central High School.*

*The detailing is all optional and dependent upon whatever doo-dads you can find lying around the house and in your craft supplies store. The sewing itself won't take very long, but the planning, gathering supplies and, yes, gluing, requires more than just a morning to complete.*

**Pants**

1.    Cut out two fronts and two backs. Note that you do not cut out the pockets on the pattern piece for the fronts. Right sides together, sew the fronts to the backs at the side seams.

2.    Cut the 3/8" wide colored grosgrain ribbon in half and center each piece over the side seams. Use a tiny zig-zag stitch to sew both sides of the ribbon down.

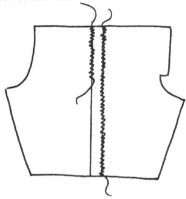

3.    Right sides together, sew the center back seam.

4.    Right sides together, sew the center front seam up to the dot. Serge or zig-zag the seam allowances separately all the way to the waist.

5.    Press left front toward inside of garment along seam line and baste at waistline. Top stitch for fly.

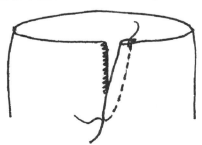

6.	Cut a strip of black twill, on grain, 1-3/4" X 13-1/4" for the waistband. Serge or zig-zag one long edge. Right sides together, and with ends of the waistband extending 1/4" beyond the pants, sew the long unfinished edge of the waistband to the pants.

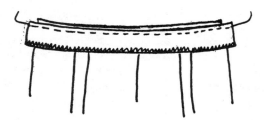

7.	Press the short ends of the waistband in and fold the whole waistband toward the inside of the garment so that the waistband is 1/2" wide. Top stitch from the right side.

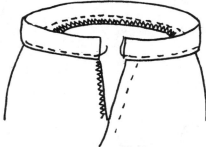

8.	Hem the pants by pressing the bottoms under 1/4" twice. Stitch.

9.	Sew the inner leg seam.

**Jacket**

1.	Cut out two fronts, two backs, two sleeves and two neck facings from the colored twill.

2.	Stitch the dart in each back.

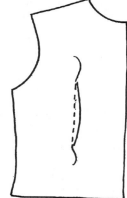

3.	Right sides together, sew the center back seam from the neckline down to the dot. Carefully press the seam allowances open from the inside of the garment. Top stitch around the back vent.

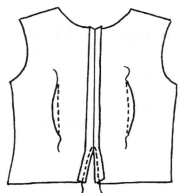

4.	Zig-zag or serge the lower edges of the jacket. Do not hem yet.

5.	Right sides together, sew fronts to back at shoulder seams.

6.	Right sides together, sew center back seam of jacket facing. Press seam allowance open. Serge or zig-zag the long inside edge of the facing as shown.

7.	Right sides together, pin jacket facing to jacket. Stitch across the lower end of the facing, up the center front and across the remaining short end of the facing. Clip corners and curves, trim seam allowances and turn right side out. Press from the wrong side.

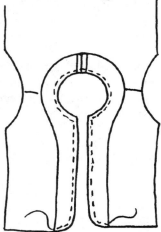

8.	Zig-zag or serge the bottom edges of the sleeves. Hem by pressing under 1/4" and hand stitching.

9.	Gather the sleeve cap slightly. Right sides together, pin to armhole of jacket. Stitch.

10. Right sides together and starting at wrist, sew sleeve and jacket underarm seam all at once. Clip curves. Turn right side out.

11. To hem, press the lower edges of the jacket under 1/4" and top stitch from beginning of the jacket facings to the center back vent.

12. Lapping right front over left by about 1/2", sew snaps in place, or use Velcro®.

**Overlay**

1. Cut out two fronts and two front shoulder pieces from white twill. Cut two backs from colored twill.

2. Right sides together, sew one white front to one colored back at the right shoulder. Sew one white front shoulder piece to the left shoulder of the colored back.

3. Cut a 1-1/4" X 8-3/4" strip from the scrap of black twill for the collar. Fold it in half lengthwise, right sides together. Stitch the short ends in a curved line as shown.

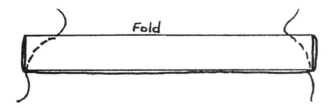

4. Clip curves, turn right side out and press. Pin the collar to the wrong side of the overlay, starting at the center front of the overlay and ending up 1/4" from the end of the white front shoulder piece. Baste.

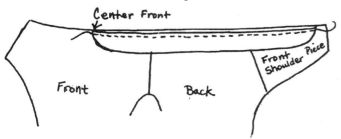

5. Sew the remaining white front, colored back and white front shoulder piece together as you did in step 2 to make the overlay lining.

6. Right sides together, place the lining over the overlay. Stitch together, starting at the short end of the front shoulder piece, going around the neckline (the collar is sandwiched between the overlay and its lining) and sewing across the left shoulder seam. Clip curves and turn right side out. Press.

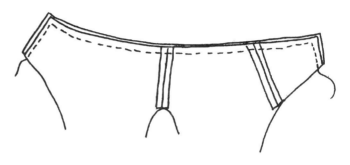

7. Press all remaining raw edges of both the overlay and its lining under 1/4" and pin together **but do not stitch yet.**

8. For the adjustable side belts, cut four strips of the 5/8" colored ribbon, each one 3" long. Tuck one between the overlay and lining on each side of the front and back as indicated on the pattern piece. Pin in place.

9. To make epaulets, use the 4" piece of 7/8" wide black ribbon. Cut an 4" long piece of 3/8" wide colored ribbon. Center the colored ribbon over the black ribbon and zig-zag along the edges of the colored ribbon. Cut a point in each end and treat the cut edges with liquid fabric sealant to prevent ravelling. Cut in half to make two epaulets.

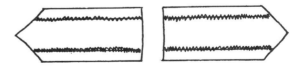

10. Tuck each epaulet between the overlay and its lining at the shoulder seam, with the right side of the striped epaulet facing the lining. Stitch all around the previously unstitched edges of the overlay. Leave the epaulets as they are for now.

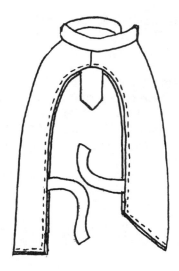

out your school's name. **This is harder than it looks** because the felt slides all over and you may end up with misshapen letters. The easiest way to do this is to cut out paper letters, apply glue to the **right side** of the paper letters with glue stick and press them face down on a piece of felt. That way the letter pattern won't "squirm" while you cut it out. Simply peel the paper away when you are done.

4. Use tacky glue to apply the school name to the wide diagonal ribbon as shown in the photograph. Duluth Central's symbol is the Trojan, which Joan made from red and black felt on the upper left part of the overlay; but her daughter Becky thought it looked like a watermelon (!). Maybe miniaturization doesn't always work out. You can try putting your school's mascot on the overlay, or leave it off.

### Customizing

Naturally your school's colors may be different from ours, and the trimming of the overlay may well also have a very different style. However, ours is a pretty typical and up-to-date style, but you will have to do your own customizing. These are only guidelines.

1. Zig-zag 5/8" wide white ribbon to the sides of the overlay back as shown. Be sure you turn the ends of the ribbon under 1/4" at the bottom and shoulder seam. Iron on black letters (1-1/2" tall) on back as shown according to your school's name. We used a D and a C for Duluth Central..

5. Make two loops of the white cording and tack it to the right shoulder seam at the outermost edge of the overlay. Fold the epaulets up over the shoulder seams so that the point is 1/4" from the black collar of the overlay. Stitch in place.

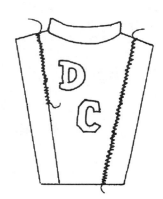

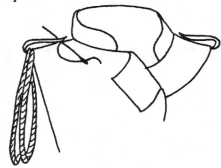

2. To trim the front of the overlay, zig-zag 3/8" wide red ribbon around it, 1/4" from the overlay's edge. You will need to fold the ends under 1/4" at the shoulder seams and miter the ribbon at the angles. Apply the 7/8" wide red ribbon diagonally, from right shoulder to lower left angle by zig-zagging both sides. Remember to fold the ends under 1/4" at shoulder seam and lower left corner.

3. Cut out 3/4" tall letters from black felt spelling

6. To complete the overlay's side belts, fold the free ends of the ribbon on the **front** overlay under 1/2", enclosing in the loop on each side the flat part of two belt loop half rings. Hand stitch securely. Use liquid sealant on the back ribbons to prevent fraying.

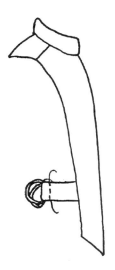

7. Sew Velcro® at left shoulder so that the front meets the back at the shoulder seam.

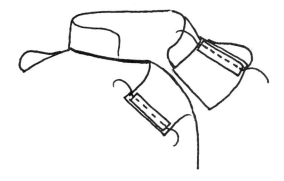

**Hat**

1. Using the pattern piece, cut an inner riser from posterboard and an outer riser from vinyl. Cut a crown from posterboard. Cut a brim from posterboard.

2. Using tacky glue, apply the wrong side of the vinyl riser to the posterboard one. The posterboard should extend beyond the vinyl 1/4" at each end.

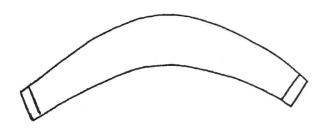

3. Overlapping the ends 1/4", glue the posterboard ends together. The vinyl ends should just meet and not overlap.

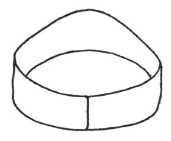

4. Cut 1/2" long slits all around the posterboard crown at 1/2" intervals. Fold the resulting notches down and apply glue to them. Place the notches of the crown inside the riser and press them so the glue makes contact all the way around.

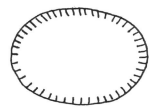 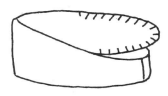

5. Invert the hat and trace the crown onto the wrong side of the vinyl. Cut out vinyl crown and glue on top of hat.

6. Cut 1/2" deep notches at 1/2" intervals around the smaller curve of the posterboard brim. Glue to the bottom of the hat front with the notches inside the hat.

7. Cut out a hat band from the red felt. Glue it to the outside of the hat riser, centering the high point over the brim. Glue the silver buttons to the riser at each end of the brim.

8. Glue the ends of the chain to the hat so that they look like they're attached to the buttons and it drapes across the brim seam. Glue white soutache braid around the top of the hat to cover the joining of crown and riser.

9. Glue the gold foil emblem to the center front of the riser. Glue a feather between the riser and the hat band at the center front if you wish.

# Overalls and Tiny T-Shirt

*Joan's daughter Becky is at that stage now when she shops for school clothes at the army surplus store-- no more fancy smocked dresses for her! Jean's daughter Maggie also prefers less formal attire. In fact, it seems like her whole class has voted for school uniforms consisting of overalls and tiny T-shirts. So here's our version for dolls.*

**Supplies for Overalls**

1/3 yd. denim fabric
4 decorative snaps, size 18
Purchased applique'
Orange Thread

**Overalls**

1.      Cut out two fronts, two backs, two front pockets, two back pockets, a strip of denim 1-1/4" X 7" (on grain) for the front waistband, and a strip 1-1/4" X 6-1/2" for the back waistband. Cut out one front bib, one back bib and two straps. For belt loops, cut a strip of denim on grain 3/4" X 6". (Yes, overalls have belt loops, crazy as it seems. If you really want to get carried away, you can add a hammer loop along one side seam.)

2.      Press the curved edges of the pocket fronts toward the wrong side 1/4".

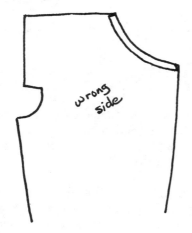

3.      Right side of pocket to wrong side of jeans, place each front pocket behind the curved edge so that the sides line up. Stitch close to the curved edge with orange thread. (This is a fake pocket, so you are stitching the top closed.) Repeat the stitching 1/8" away, or use twin needle to get double stitching effect.

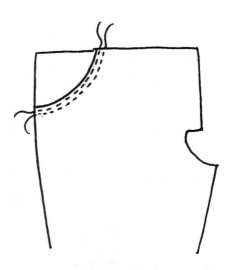

4.      Right sides together, sew fronts together at center seam **only up to the dot marked on the pattern piece.** Press the right fly extension 1/8" toward the wrong side and stitch.

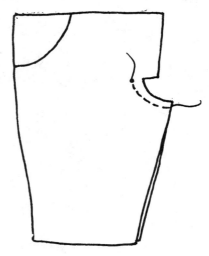

5.      Fold left fly toward the inside of the jeans along the center front seam line. Stitch along stitching line as marked as two rows on the pattern piece. Also stitch reinforcements as shown.

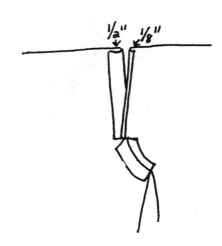

14

6. Press all edges of back pockets under 1/4". With orange thread, stitch along the top edge of each pocket, 1/8" from the folded edge. Pin in place on jeans backs as indicated on the pattern piece. Using double stitching, sew all edges except the top to the jeans.

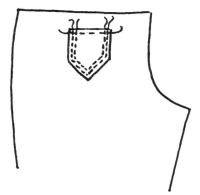

7. Right sides together, sew center back seam.

8. Right sides together, sew side seams from bottom edge **up to 1/2" below the side pocket stitching.**

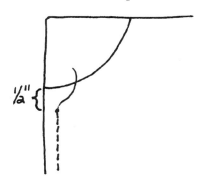

9. Right sides together, sew the front waistband to the pants front. Press open.

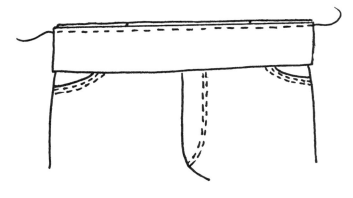

10. Press the two sides and top edge of the front bib 1/4" toward the wrong side to hem it. Top stitch the edges with two rows of stitching.

11. Right sides together, center the front bib on the front waistband and stitch. Press the remaining part of the front waistband toward the wrong side and sides of waistband and unstitched seam area and top stitch.

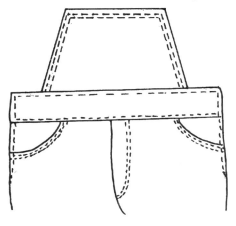

12. Right sides together, sew the back waistband to the pants back and press open.

13. Press the two sides and top edge of the back bib 1/4" toward the wrong side to hem it. Top stitch the edges with two rows of stitching.

14. Right sides together, center the back bib on the back waistband and stitch. Press open. Press remaining part of waistband, sides of waistband and unstitched seam area.

15. Press the long edges and shortest end of the straps 1/4" toward the wrong side. Top stitch with one row of stitching.

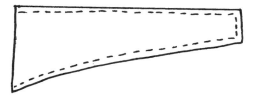

16. Place the wide end of each strap underneath the back bib edge so that the sides touch. Stitch in place.

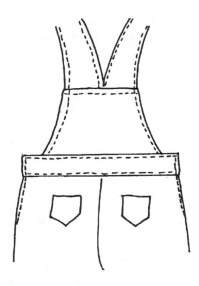

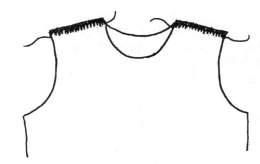

3. Sew the short ends of the ribbing together to make a circle.

4. Fold the ribbing in half lengthwise, wrong sides together.

5. Stretching the ribbing to fit the neck, serge or zig-zag to neck opening.

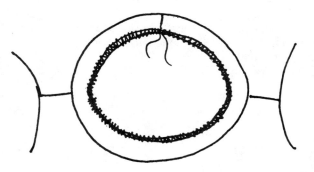

6. Serge or zig-zag the bottom edges of the sleeves. Press under 1/4" and top stitch.

7. Right sides together, serge or zig-zag sleeves to shirt armholes. Serge or zig-zag underarm seam, starting at sleeve hem and finishing at the waistline.

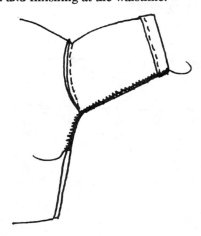

8. Hem the lower edge of the shirt by serging or zig-zagging the raw edge, then turning it under 1/4". Top stitch.

17. To hem, press the lower edges of the jeans under 1/4" twice. Top stitch with orange thread.

18. Right sides together, sew inner leg seam.

19. To make belt loops, narrow hem the long edges of the 3/4" X 6" strip so that it ends up being 1/4" wide. Cut it into four 1-1/2" lengths. Press the short ends of each loop under 1/4" and topstitch in place as indicated on the pattern piece.

20. Using fusible web or fabric glue, center applique' on front bib.

21. Apply snaps, following manufacturer's instructions, to top of front bib and straps and sides at waistband, overlapping front over back 1/2".

# Tiny T-Shirt

**Supplies for T-Shirt**

1/4 yd. T-shirt type interlock knit fabric
    (with horizontal stretch)
2" knit ribbing

1. Cut out one front, one back, and two sleeves from the interlock knit fabric. Cut a piece of ribbing 8" X 1-1/2" for the neck.

2. Right sides together, sew the shoulder seams with serger or zig-zag stitch.

# Soccer Uniform

*This is really a quick and easy outfit. We noticed there's a great variety of shirt styles among soccer players. Oftentimes the younger kids simply get plain T-shirts with large numbers applied on the back. School teams usually have a V-shaped neckline with contrasting trim, and that's the style we chose.*

<u>Supplies</u>

1/4 yd. knit or athletic mesh fabric
    for shirt
1/8 yd. contrasting nylon tricot for trim
1/4 yd. Gortex®, knit or poplin for
    shorts
12" contrasting grosgrain or satin ribbon
    (1/2" wide) for stripes on shorts
12" elastic (1/4" wide)
13" elastic (1/8" wide)
Scrap of heavy weight interfacing
    for shin guards
soccer ball applique'
1-1/2" tall iron-on number for shirt

**Shorts**

1. Cut out two fronts and two backs. Right sides together, sew center back and center front seams.

2. Sew side seams from waistline only down to dot marked on pattern piece. Press entire seam allowance open for each seam. Top stitch around the side slit.

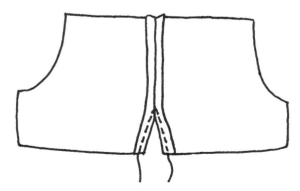

3. Pin ribbon stripes over side seams, making the ribbon flush with the waistline of the shorts and ending at the dot. Press the end of the ribbon under 1/4" before you pin it in place at the dot so that the ribbon end does not fray later.

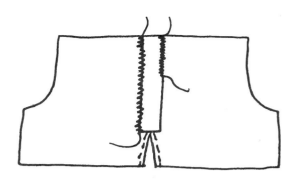

4. To hem the shorts, press under the bottom edge 1/4" twice and top stitch.

5. To make the elastic casing in the waistline, press the edge under 1/4", then another 1/2". Stitch along the folded edge, leaving an opening at the center back to insert elastic. Run the 1/4" elastic through the casing with a tapestry needle or bodkin. Machine stitch the ends of the elastic together where it best fits your doll's waist. Machine stitch the opening to completely enclose the elastic.

**Shirt**

1. Cut out one front, one back and two sleeves from the knit or mesh fabric.

2. From the contrasting tricot (we found regular knit ribbing to be too bulky for this), cut four strips 1-1/4" X 6-1/2", one for the neck front and one for the neck back, plus one for each sleeve, so that the stretch is horizontal.

3. To finish off the sleeves, fold two of the tricot strips in half lengthwise, wrong sides together. Pin the folded tricot strip to the bottom of each sleeve, on the right side, and stitch. You may want to serge or zig-zag the seam allowances. Press the tricot trim down.

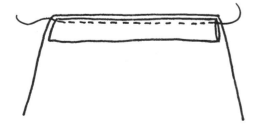

4. Apply a folded tricot strip the same way to the back neckline of the shirt. You will have to clip the seam allowance around the curves.

5. For the front V-shaped neckline, fold the tricot trim in half lengthwise, and then crosswise to mark the center front. Make a mitered 45-degree corner and stitch. Trim seam.

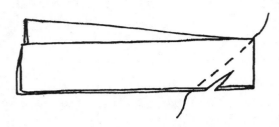

6. Pin the V-shaped trim to the right side of the shirt front and stitch, pivoting on the machine needle at the center front point. Press open.

7. Right sides together, sew front to back at shoulder seams.

8. Run a gathering stitch around the sleeve caps and adjust the gathers slightly to fit the shirt armhole. Stitch.

9. Right sides together, and in one motion, sew underarm seam, starting at sleeve edge and ending up at lower edge of the shirt.

10. Hem the shirt by pressing the lower edge 1/4" toward the inside of the garment. Stitch.

11. Apply the soccer ball applique' to the left side of the shirt with fusable web. Iron on the number to the shirt back.

**Shin Guards**

1. Cut six from heavy interfacing. Sew three together for each guard, stitching 1/8" from all edges. Draw vertical lines as shown on the pattern piece and stitch.

2. Cut two pieces of 1/8" elastic, each 3-1/2" long. Sew the ends to the inside top of each guard as shown on the pattern piece. Cut two pieces of elastic, each 3" long, and sew them to the lower inside as indicated on the pattern.

# Letter Jacket and Blue Jeans

*This jacket is a duplicate of the one earned by Jean's son Matt, who attends The Marshall School. Daughter Maggie plans to earn her own letter jacket in volleyball. We were astonished to find the perfect color of leather at a leather and crafts chain store and matching snaps at a regular fabric shop. This pattern could easily be used to make an all black or brown leather bomber jacket. To do that, stitch diagonal lines for fake pockets and substitute a small separating zipper for snaps.*

### Supplies for Letter Jacket

1/4 yd. black wool fabric
Scrap of colored leather
    soft enough to sew
3" black ribbing
5 decorative snaps
    5/16" wide, same color
    as leather
Scrap of sticky-back felt
    same color as leather
    or purchased sticky-back
    felt letter (1-1/4" tall)
leather needle for sewing machine
fabric glue stick

### Letter Jacket

1. Cut out one back and two fronts from the wool fabric. If you plan to machine or hand embroider a name on the right front, do so **before you cut it out**, following placement on the pattern piece.

2. Cut out the collar from the ribbing using the pattern.

3. Cut out two sleeves from the leather. Cut a piece of ribbing 2-1/2" X 13" for the jacket waistline. Cut two pieces of ribbing, each 1-1/4" X 3-1/2" for the sleeve cuffs.

4. Right sides together, sew jacket fronts to back at shoulders.

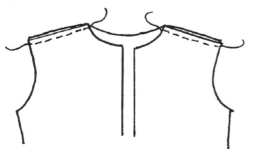

5. Zig-zag or serge the center front edges and fold towards the inside of the garment along the fold line indicated on the pattern piece. Hand baste in place along the top and bottom edges of the center front.

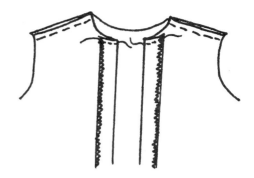

6. Fold the collar ribbing in half lengthwise, right sides together, so that the curved edge is at each center front. Stitch curve. Turn right side out.

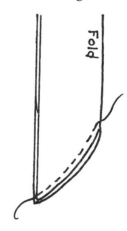

7. Pin the folded collar around the neckline of the jacket, on the right side. Zig-zag.

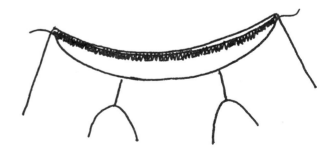

8. Using the leather needle, gather the sleeve cap with one row of long stitches. Pull the gathering threads slightly to fit the jacket armholes. Right sides together, **on the seam allowances only**, use fabric glue stick to hold the sleeve in place (it's too hard to pin through the leather, and you want to minimize pinholes anyway). Stitch.

9. Fold cuff ribbing in half lengthwise, right sides out. Stretch the cuffs to fit the lower edge of each sleeve and zig-zag or serge.

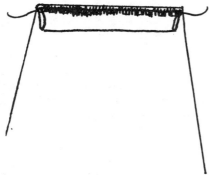

10. Right sides together, sew the underarm seam from wrist to waist.

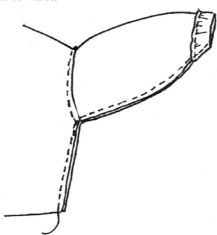

11. Fold the waistline ribbing in half lengthwise, **wrong** sides out, and stitch the short ends. Turn right side out and pin it to the right side of the bottom of the jacket. Zig-zag or serge. Press ribbing down.

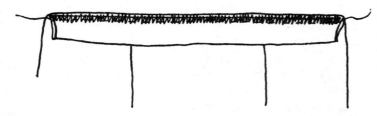

12. Apply school's initial letter to left front of jacket as indicated on the pattern piece. If you bought a letter or felt that is sticky-back, and a child will actually play with this garment, we advise that you use some extra fabric glue or embroider it in place for durability.

13. Using the appropriate snap fastening device for your brand of snaps, apply the decorative part of the snaps to the right front and the rest of the snaps to the left front. Place one snap in the waistline ribbing and space the rest at 1" intervals.

# Blue Jeans

### Supplies for Blue Jeans

1/3 yd. denim fabric
1 decorative snap, size 14
Orange thread

### Blue Jeans

1. Cut out two fronts, two backs, two front pockets, two back pockets and a strip of denim 1-1/2" X 13" (on grain) for the waistband. For belt loops, cut a strip of denim on grain 3/4" X 6".

2. Press the curved edges of the center fronts toward the wrong side 1/4" (along center front seam lines).

3. Right side of pocket to wrong side of jeans, place each front pocket behind the curved edge so that the sides line up. Stitch close to the curved edge with orange thread. (This is a fake pocket so you are stitching the top closed.) Repeat the stitching 1/8" away, or use twin needle to get double stitching effect.

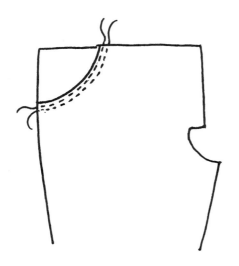

4. Right sides together, sew fronts together at center seam **only up to the dot marked on the pattern piece.** Press the right fly edge 1/8" toward the wrong side and stitch.

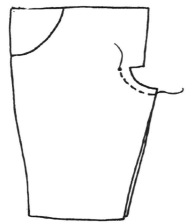

5. Fold left fly toward the inside of the jeans along the center front seam line. Stitch along stitching line as marked on the pattern piece. Also stitch reinforcements as shown.

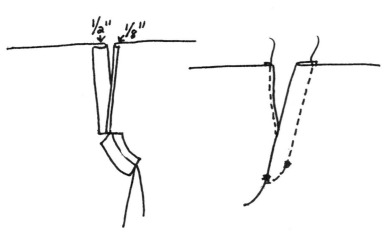

6. Press all edges of back pockets under 1/4". With orange thread, stitch along the top edge of each pocket, 1/8" from the folded edge. Pin in place on jeans backs as indicated on the pattern piece. Using double stitching, sew all edges except the top to the jeans.

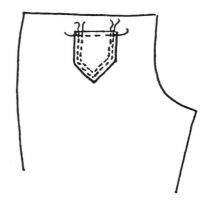

7. Right sides together, sew side seams.

8. Serge or zig-zag along one long edge of the waistband. Right sides together, and with ends extending 1/4" beyond the center fronts of the jeans, sew the long unfinished edge of the waistband to the jeans.

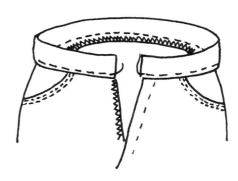

9. Fold the waistband over into the inside of the garment so that the waistband is 1/2" wide, tucking in the short ends. Topstitch in place.

10. To hem, press the lower edges of the jeans under 1/4" twice. Top stitch with orange thread.

11. Right sides together, sew inner leg seam.

12. To make belt loops, narrow hem the long edges of the 3/4" X 6" strip so that it ends up being 1/4" wide. Cut it into four 1-1/2" lengths. Press the short ends of each loop under 1/4" and topstitch in place as indicated on the pattern piece.

Pattern Pieces for
**Action Wear for Dolls**
by
Joan Hinds and Jean Becker

Copyright 1996 by
Fancywork and Fashion Press

Because this is a set of patterns bound into a book, we recommend that you trace the pattern pieces you need onto thin typing paper and keep them in a separate envelope. Several pieces are used in more than one design, so be careful to use the correct cutting lines for the outfit you are working on. As usual, note when patterns are to be placed on a fold. And one final reminder: the seam allowances are 1/4" and are already accounted for on each pattern piece.

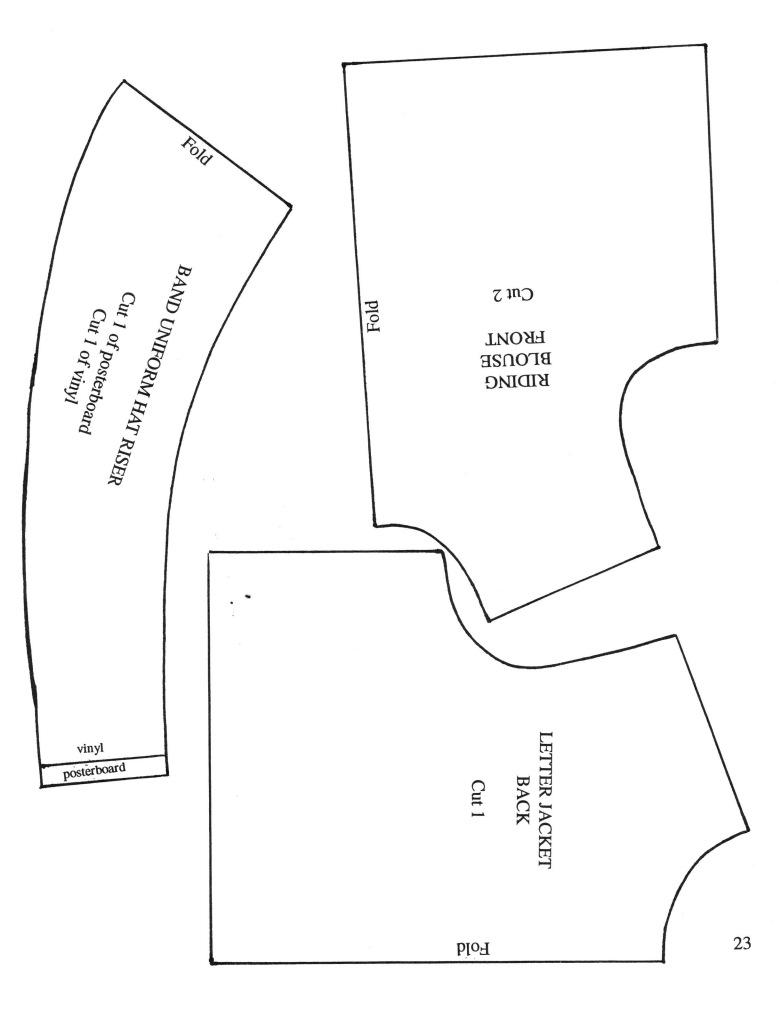

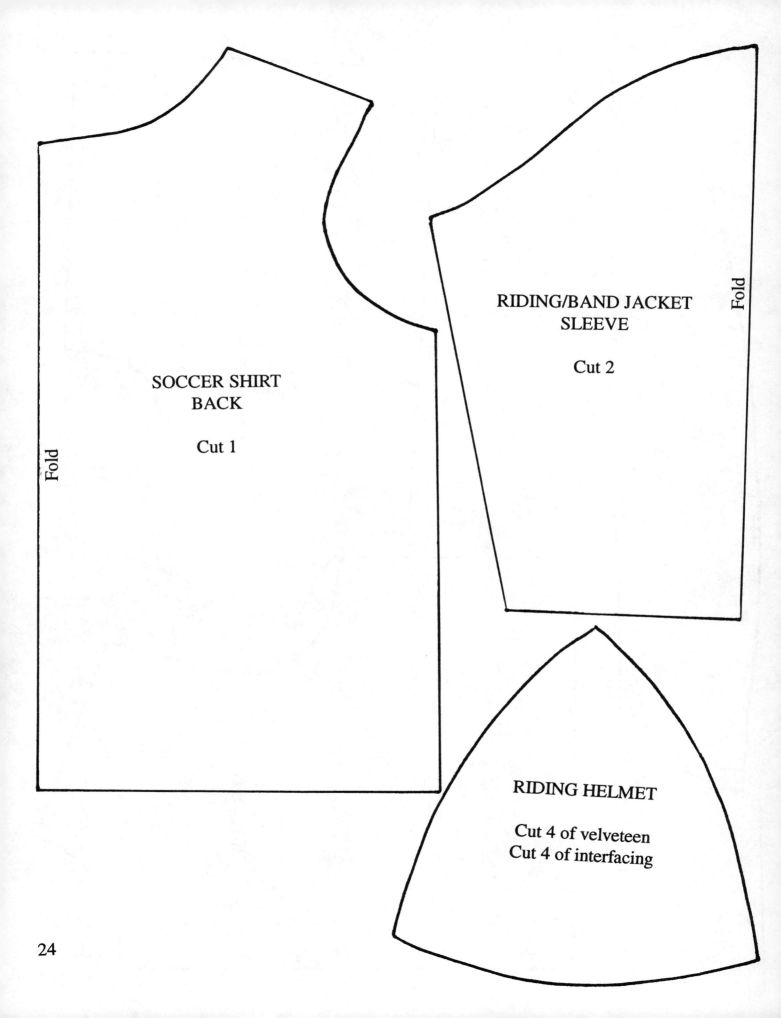

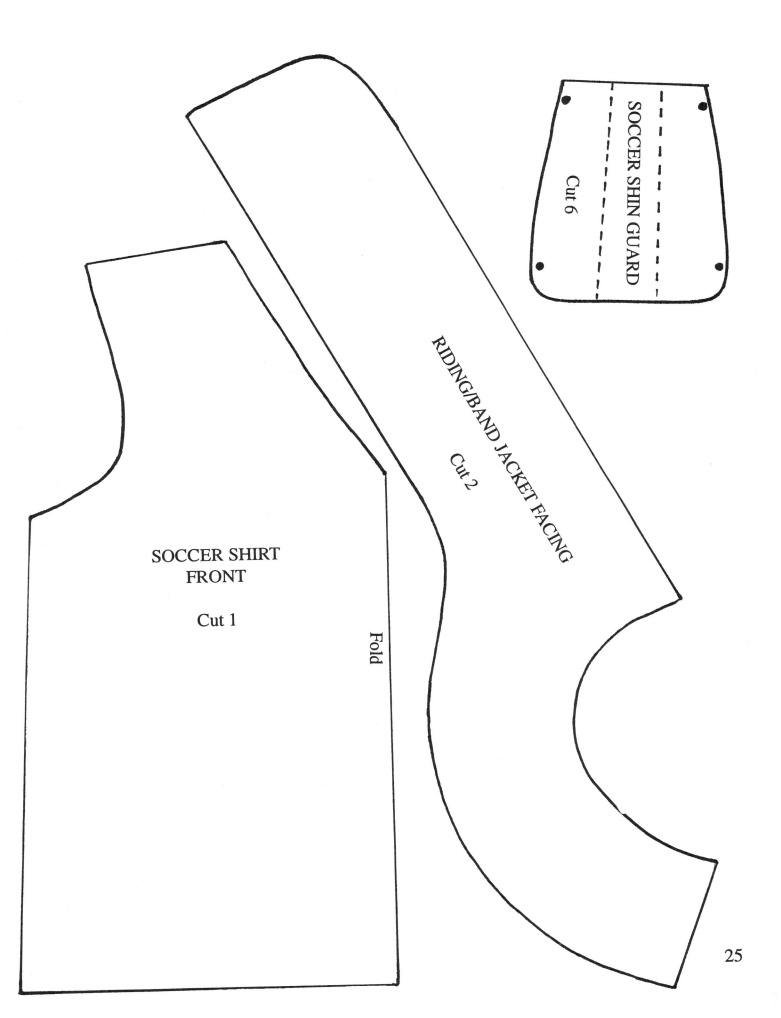

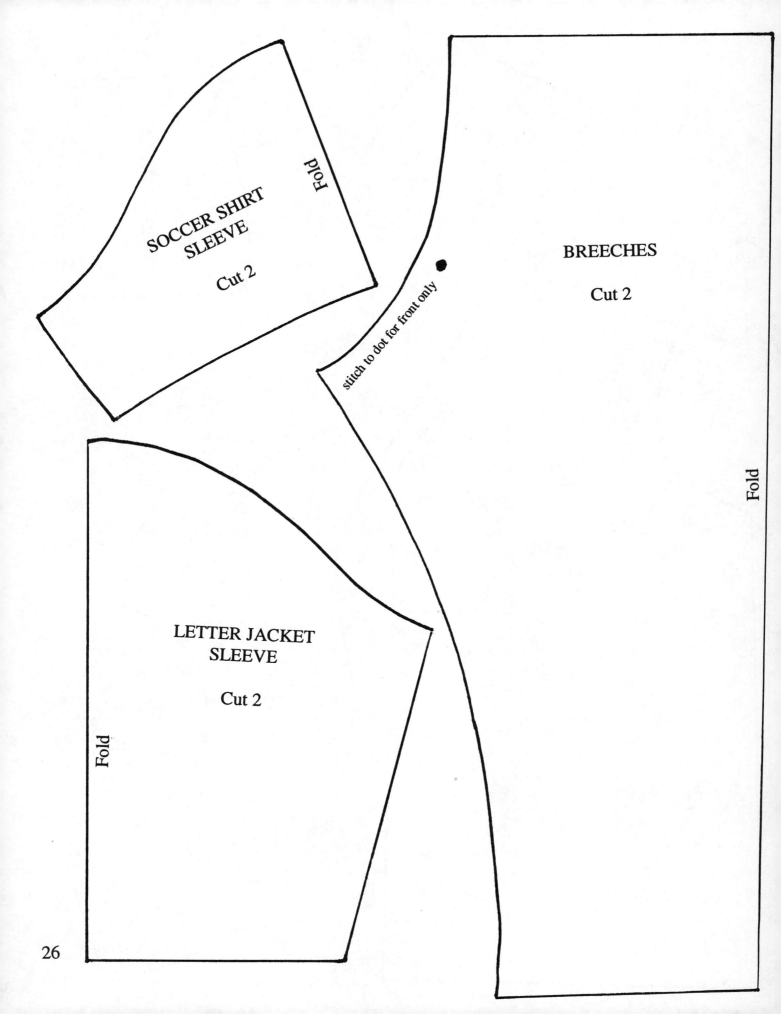

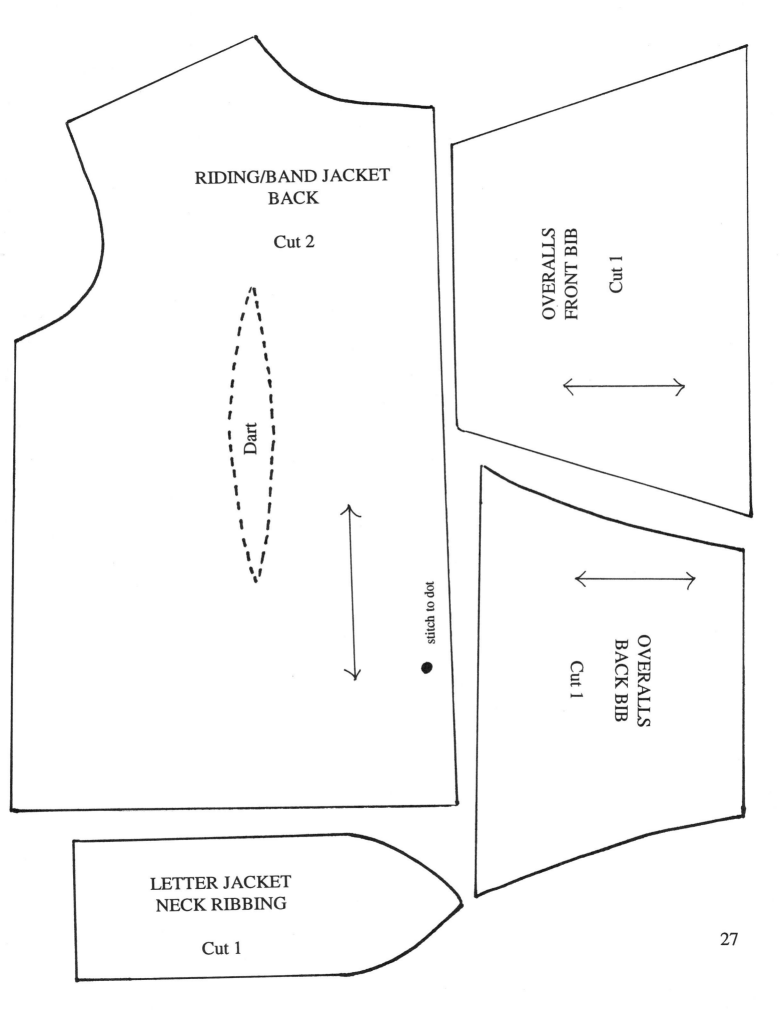

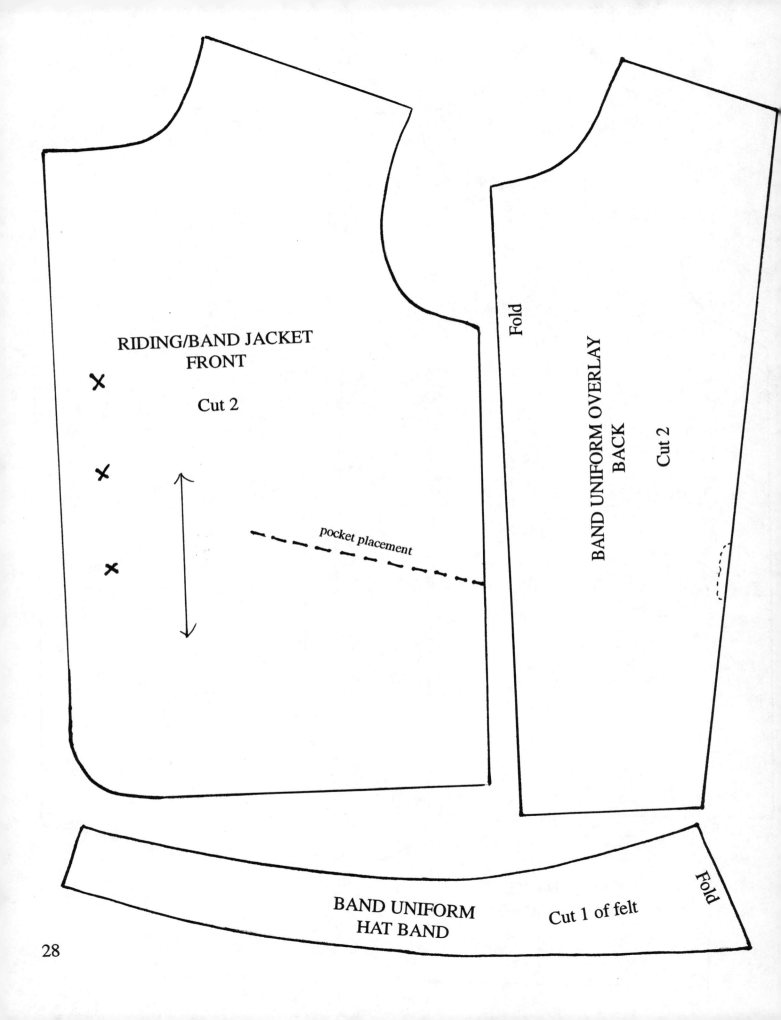

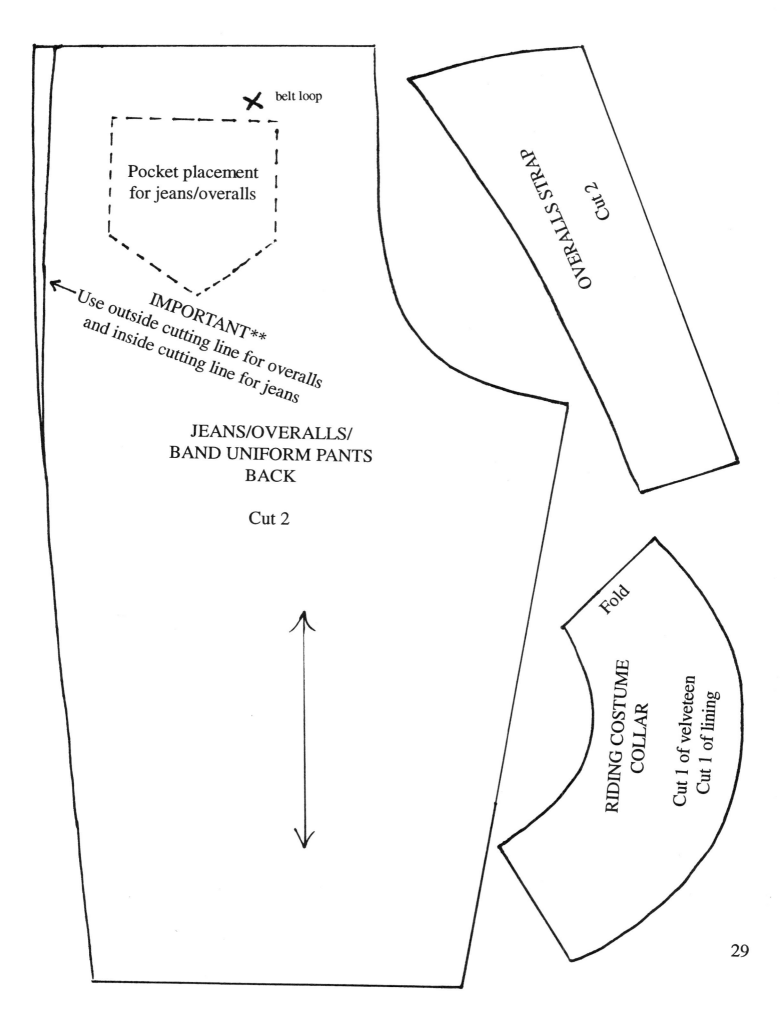

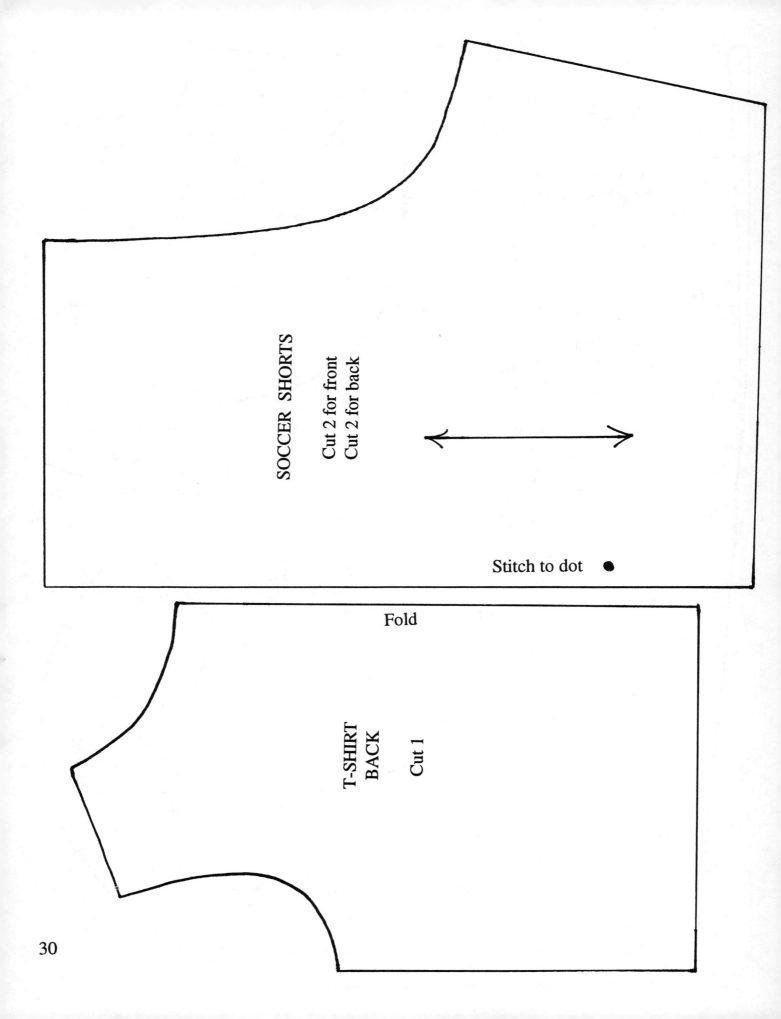

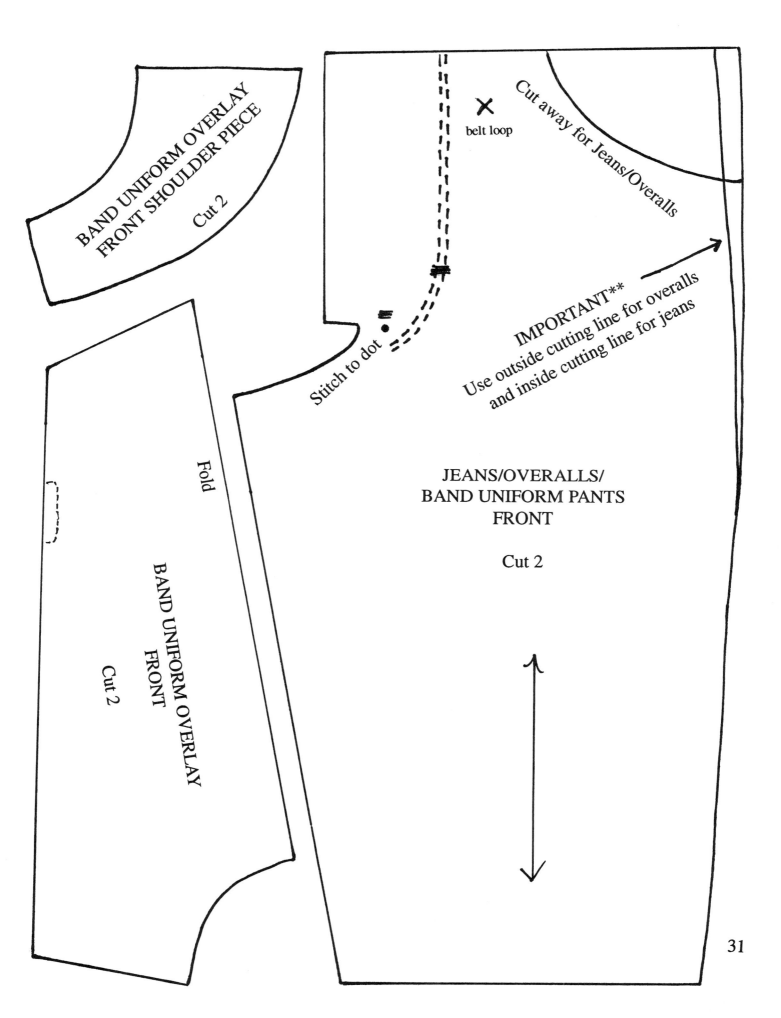

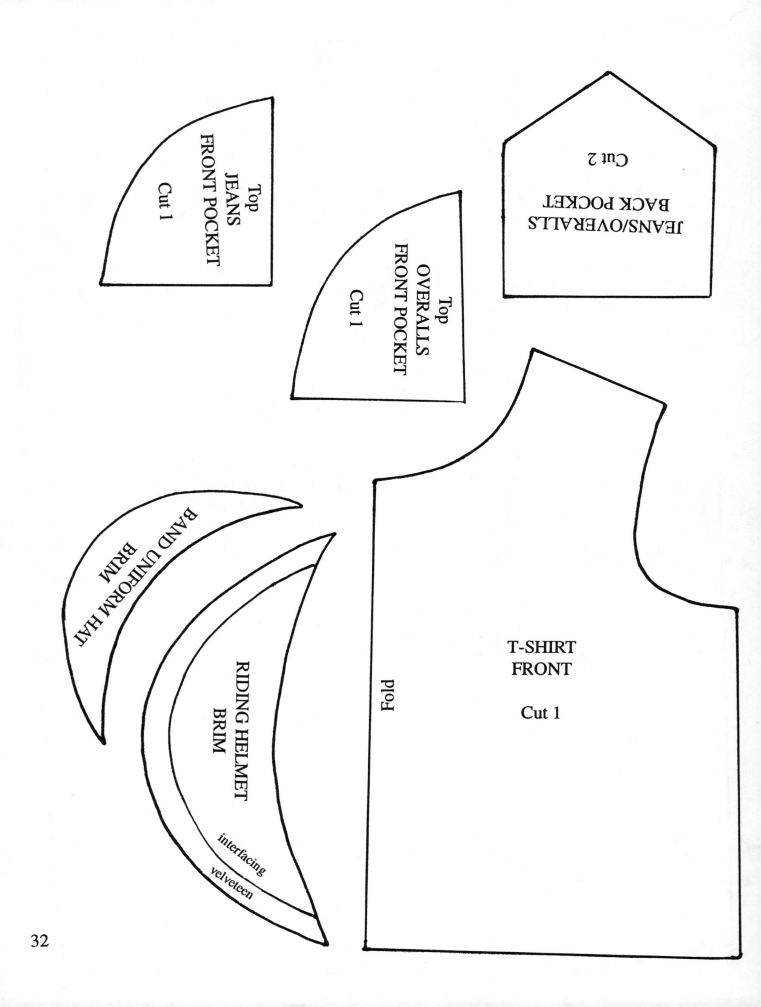

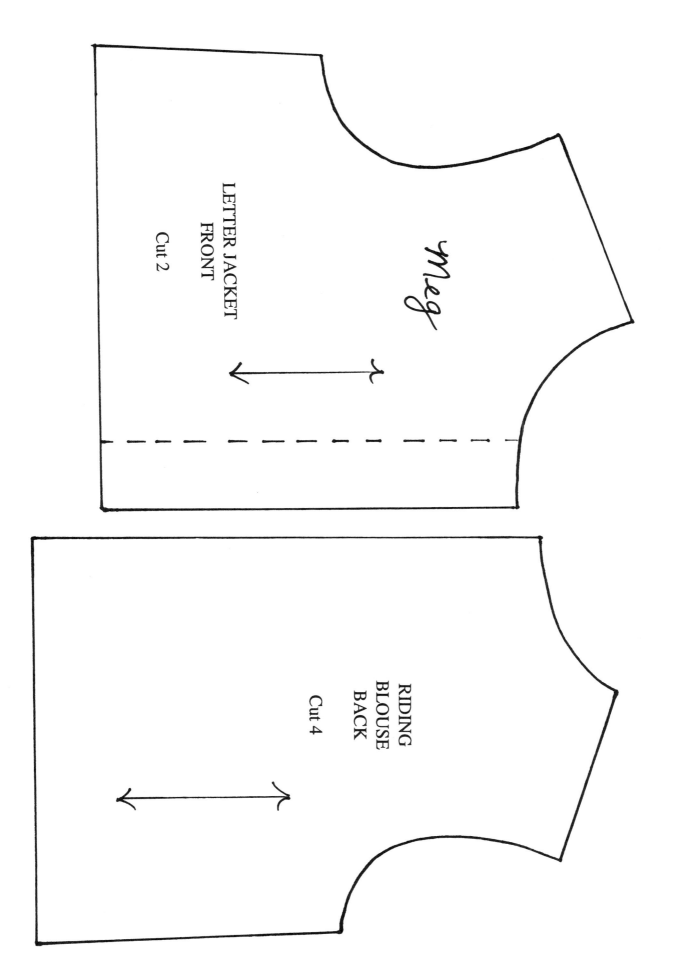

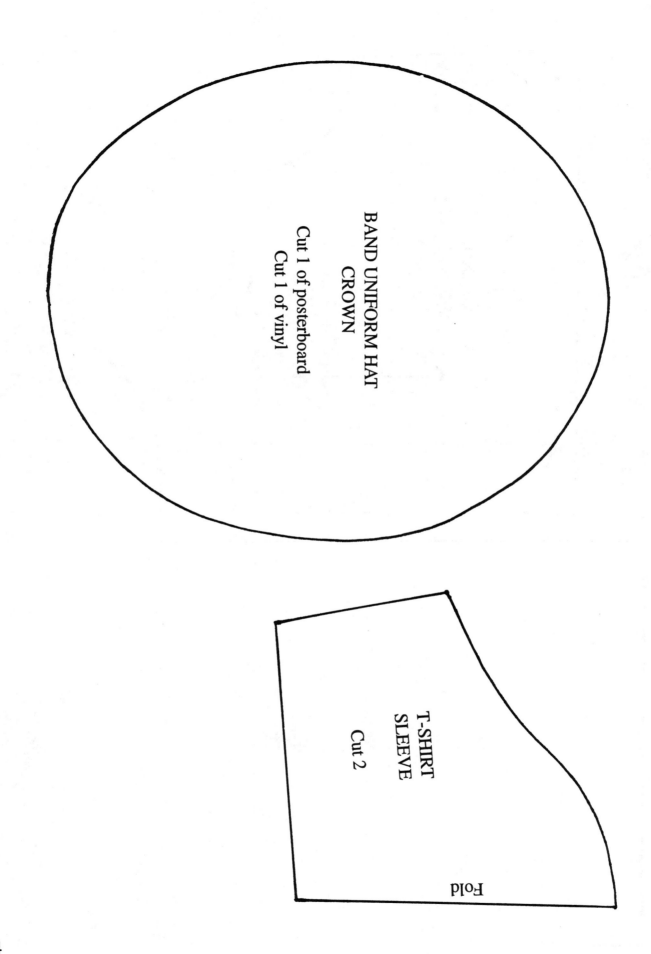

## CREDITS

All dolls used as models in this book are by Götz Dolls®, a German company. The dolls are found in fine toy stores all over the U.S.

The shoes and boots are available through several mail order companies, which advertise in doll and sewing magazines, as well as dolls shops.

Miniature musical instruments are available through various mail order catalogs specializing in music-related items, as well as in doll and toy shops.

## About the Authors

Joan Hinds and Jean Becker have been creative partners since 1989. Their four previous costuming books have become classics among those who sew for dolls. Well known for patterns that are easy to follow and actually fit, they have specialized in 18" modern vinyl dolls such as Götz and American Girls by Pleasant Company®. Their <u>Best Doll Clothes Book</u>, now in its third printing, is often recommended as "the one set of patterns you cannot do without."

When they aren't packing orders in their mail order warehouse or dreaming up new patterns, they are busy with their families.

Joan and her husband Fletcher have two children, Kevin, age 17, and Becky, age 14. Try not to say the phrase "driver's license" around Joan. The Hinds household reflects Joan's training in interior design and a life-long interest in art.

Jean and her husband Terrence have three children: Matt, age 15, Maggie, age 12 and Max, age 10. They also have two Irish wolfhounds (that's 260 pounds of dog) and three cats. Try not to say "hairball" around Jean.

For current information about books in print by these authors, send a long, self-addressed envelope with two first class stamps to:

**Fancywork and Fashion Press**
**4728 Dodge Street**
**Duluth, MN 55804**